Annabel Sutton, BA (Hons), ACC

Since 2000, Annabel has worked as a Personal Life Coach, inspiring people to make positive changes – and to find increased happiness and success in their personal and professional lives. She runs several coaching programmes, including 'Springclean Your Life', 'Manage Your Time – Manage Your Life' and 'Business Success for Women' – an inspirational group programme for women at the early stages of setting up a business.

Annabel grew up in England but has lived in Los Angeles, Borneo and Java and is the author of "*The Islands in Between*" a travel book she researched and wrote while living in Indonesia. She now lives with her partner Don in Cheshire and is passionate about organic gardening, wildlife, good food and laughter – not necessarily in that order!

Coaching

If this book inspires you to want to make positive changes in your life, you might like to find out how coaching could support you. For further information, or to arrange a complimentary consultation (either in person or over the phone) please call 01625 584518.

If you would like to receive Annabel's Coaching Tips on a regular basis, please call the above number, or send an email to annabel@life-designs.co.uk

You can also visit Annabel's website at www.life-designs.co.uk

52 Ways to Handle It

A Life Coaching Year

Annabel Sutton

For Joy —
wishing you inspiration
and fun in 2005 —

Annabel Sutton

Winter Press
16 Stambourne Way
West Wickham
Kent BR4 9NF
e-mail: winterpress@hotmail.com

First published by Winter Press in 2003

© Annabel Sutton

ISBN 1 874581 52 5

Printed by Biddles of Guildford, Surrey

What e-Tips' Readers Say...

Annabel is like a breath of fresh air. She challenges conventional ways and attitudes and makes you see things in a different light.
Sheelagh Ward, Independent Nursing Consultant

Annabel's tips provide laser like clarity to fuzzy thinking – she can make even the most daunting task manageable and achievable, hence huge satisfaction when her tips are put into action.
Annabel Burton, Astrologer

In the hectic quest for success, your Coaching Tips have been a welcome hand on the shoulder asking me to pause, take a deep breath and recognise the wealth that already surrounds me. They do what every good friend does – look out for the well being of those around them in a helpful, practical way.
Harry Owen

These tips really provide practical and easy to follow steps to handle the stuff that often gets in the way of how we want things to be. They are easy to apply which means that they really work and make an immediate difference. Simply wonderful.
Ali Giblin, Career & Business Coach

Annabel's coaching tips are original and practical. They give me a focus and have helped me to overcome the every day challenges that life throws up.
Blaire Palmer, Managing Director

Your tips have been my weekly calming fix amid a chaotic year.
Val Lipworth

The wonderful thing about your tips: We knew these pearls all along. But without your reminding us, they would have stayed way down there on the ocean floor. Thanks!

Helyn Connor

Annabel's coaching tips bring a breath of fresh air on many a hot day. If I need something to remind me to focus on the key issues in my life I have found that they often hit the nail on the head.

Stephen G Baker, Private Banker with HBOS

After I've read Annabel's tips I always find myself asking the question "now why didn't I think of that?" because they're all such common sense!

Ara Couligian

There is a quiet steadfastness about her advice that seems to encourage my little-used ability to come out as the person I am and live and work with enjoyment.

Jostein Stokkeland, Language Adviser with the Norwegian Language Council

Annabel's inspiring tips have enabled me to realise that there really is an exciting life out there – a journey full of opportunities and experiences and that it really is OK to 'go for it!'.

Sarah Dawson, Reflexologist

Your tips are like having a best friend – they bring your life back into focus, they encourage you to tackle challenging issues quickly and they boost your confidence. In short, they help you make the most of life.

Jane Bleakley

Acknowledgments

So many people have been instrumental in helping me to make this book a reality.

First and foremost I want to thank Don Hartridge – not only my partner in life, but also my tireless Tips Editor-In-Chief. Every week I bash out a new Tip and take it to Don for his perusal. Not only is he great at correcting the language, but he also has a built-in Naffometer which bursts into life when I incline to go over the top, or start using too much coaching jargon!

Thanks also to my coach Margaret Krigbaum for giving me the idea of writing the book in the first place. Several months ago she did that very 'coachly' thing of delicately 'planting the seed of an idea' in my mind that perhaps writing would be a good thing. As seeds do, it slowly germinated and now, many months later, has grown into the book you are reading.

Where would I be without my marvellous family – my parents, brother and sister – who, from the moment I was born, have loved and supported and encouraged me to be who I am and be my best. I particularly owe so much to my father who had the innate talent to write, but due to life circumstances found himself on a very different career path. How pleased he would have been to know that his love of and talent for writing are living on in me.

And finally to my many colleagues in the coaching community – who are a consistently loving, supportive and inspiring influence. And to my wonderful clients who are a joy to work with and who teach me new things about life every day

Contents

Dedication

This book is dedicated with love to Eve Sutton – my Mum and my best friend.

About this Book

In 2001 I started writing a weekly Coaching Tips email, initially for my clients, and subsequently for anyone who expressed an interest in personal development. My hope was that at the start of the week, each person would receive something that might help to shape their week and energize them in the days to come – perhaps inspire them to do things differently – focus them on the positive - or change their perspective and get them thinking in a different way.

They have become immensely popular - and it struck me that it would be a good idea to publish a compilation of fifty-two tips, so that readers would have a whole year's worth, to dip into at will or to read each week, as they wish.

Whichever method you choose, the main thing is to enjoy the stimulus to thought and action that each tip provides.

Each tip has space on the opposite page for you to write your thoughts or plans of action. Or you may prefer to buy a journal or notebook to use week by week alongside this book.

I've loved writing the tips, and greatly enjoy the feedback from readers when something has struck a chord and clearly made a difference to their lives. I hope that you, too, will find them inspirational and I wish you great success and happiness in all that you undertake.

Annabel Sutton

"The only way to discover the limits of
the possible is to go beyond them
into the impossible."

Arthur C. Clarke

1. Believe the Impossible

Anything is possible. Very often the only person to place limits on our success is ourselves. Sometimes you have to dream the impossible and then truly believe it in order to galvanize yourself to take the necessary steps to make it happen.

Here's a great quote to ponder on:

> "I can't believe that!" said Alice. "One can't believe impossible things."
>
> "I daresay you haven't had much practice," said the Queen. "When I was your age, I always did it for half-an-hour a day. Why, sometimes I've believed as many as six impossible things before breakfast."
>
> (Lewis Carroll, Through the Looking Glass)

There are two lessons here. Firstly, how crucial it is to take the time to think, dream and plan – you can't think creatively when you're rushed off your feet. Secondly, to think big – to embrace the impossible.

In the '80s I climbed Mount Kinabalu in Malaysia. This wasn't a mountain climb in terms of using ropes and crampons – but, rather, 13,500 exhausting feet of ascending rough steps that had been carved into the mountain. For me, who is not naturally athletic, this feat was impossible in itself, but half way up I was overtaken by a young man who was undertaking the record for RUNNING up the mountain. Not only that, but this man had prosthetic feet. He, truly, had dreamed the impossible – and achieved it (see also Tip 5).

Is there something you have long dreamed of doing, having or being, but others have told you it was impossible?

Could this be the year that you set out to achieve it?

"People who have no time don't think.
The more you think,
the more time you have."

Henry Ford

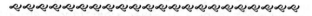

2. Four Steps to Freedom

This is one for the beginning of the year (or academic year if that's how your life is organised).

How many of us – particularly those who own our own businesses – have to admit that holidays and free time are often pushed aside by the pressures of work?

If we don't plan in advance, more often than not our 'free' time gets squeezed out, and work takes priority, leaving us desperately in need of enough time to refresh and rejuvenate – and wondering why we're feeling so stressed.

Why not make this the year when you turn that on its head and plan everything around YOU?! It couldn't be simpler:

Step One: Buy your diary, organiser or planner for the year.

Step Two: Choose four coloured pens, pencils or highlighters.

Step Three: Divide your time into four categories:

> Holidays
>
> Free time = free time when you're not away on holiday
>
> Admin time = time when you're doing all those things connected with your work (eg: accounts, marketing, research)
>
> Work time = when you're doing what you get paid for doing

Step Four: Decide how many days you want to spend in each category, and – STARTING WITH HOLIDAYS and free time – colour code your diary accordingly. You will be surprised how much more in control you feel and how good it feels to be starting the year with all your holidays and free time planned in advance.

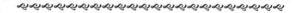

"In order to be utterly happy, the only
thing necessary is to refrain from
comparing this moment with other
moments in the past, which I often did
not fully enjoy because I was comparing
them with other moments of the future."

André Gide

3. Treasure The Present

"Imagine a bank which credits your account each morning with £86,400. It does not carry a balance over from day to day, nor does it allow you to keep any cash balance and every evening cancels whatever part of the amount you have failed to use during the day. What would you do? Draw out every penny, of course!

Well, everybody has such a bank – its name is TIME. Every morning it credits you with 86,400 seconds. Every night it writes off as lost whatever of this you have failed to invest to good purpose.

> To realise the value of ONE YEAR ask a student who has failed a grade.
>
> To realise the value of ONE MONTH ask a mother who has given birth to a premature baby.
>
> To realise the value of ONE DAY ask an editor of a weekly newspaper.
>
> To realise the value of ONE MINUTE ask a person who has just missed a train.
>
> To realise the value of ONE SECOND ask a person who has avoided an accident.
>
> To realise the value of ONE MILLI-SECOND ask the person who has won a silver medal in the Olympics.

Treasure every moment you have.

> *Yesterday is history – Tomorrow is a mystery – Today is a gift.*
> *That is why it is called the PRESENT."*
>   *(Author unknown)*

Have a great week – 604,800 seconds and counting...!

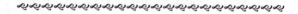

"Within you there is a stillness
and sanctuary to which you can retreat
at anytime and be yourself."

The Dhammapada

4. Great Beginnings

How do you start your day? I know how easy it is to get straight out of bed and step right onto the hamster wheel – with barely enough time to grab a piece of toast and a quick cup of coffee before you rush headlong into the day.

The way in which you start your day sets you up for what's ahead – and starting it well can make all the difference. I appreciate that if you have young children this tip might be a bit of a stretch – but see if there's still a way to carve out some 'me' time and get your day off to a great start after they have been attended to.

If you were to design the perfect start to your day, what would it look like? Would you ...

Sit down with a steaming cup of freshly brewed coffee and a croissant and read the paper in peace...

Go out for a gentle stroll, listen to the bird song and take the time to rejoice in the things around you...

Spend fifteen minutes reading an inspirational book, or listening to an inspirational tape...

Go to the gym, or do some high-energy, aerobic exercise...

Spend ten minutes doing absolutely nothing ... allow yourself to daydream ...

If you were to take the time – and make the conscious effort – to start your day off well, what difference do you think it would make?

"Men often become what they
believe themselves to be. If I
believe I cannot do something, it
makes me incapable of doing it.
But when I believe I can, then I
acquire the ability to do it even if
I didn't have it in the beginning."

Mahatma Gandhi

5. Are You Playing a Big Enough Game?

Last weekend I went down to a concert at the Albert Hall. Nothing special about that, you might think. BUT – this wasn't a concert with the BBC Symphony or even a big name like Eric Clapton (showing my age!). It was a couple of guys called Steve Knightley and Phil Beer who are usually much more at home performing in small village halls somewhere in deepest Devon.

As the duo 'Show of Hands', Phil and Steve are well known on the acoustic folk scene and are two exceptionally talented musicians and song writers who travel the country giving concerts in pubs, village halls and school assembly halls.

But last year they decided to do something really whacky. They decided that they'd take a gamble and hire the Albert Hall and see if they could fill it!

Mad, everyone said. You'll never do it, everyone said. It will be a financial and a PR disaster, everyone said.

Last Saturday the Albert Hall was packed to the roof with stamping, roaring, ecstatic music lovers and Phil and Steve had made it happen. They decided to play a MUCH BIGGER GAME and with a carefully orchestrated strategy of countrywide tours, intense PR and internet presence, they managed to fulfil their unique dream.

ARE YOU PLAYING A BIG ENOUGH GAME??!

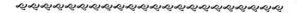

"The way to develop the best
that is in a person is by
appreciation and
encouragement."

Charles Schwab

6. When In Doubt, Add Helium!

One of the most important ingredients in creating a successful life is remembering to appreciate others.

Imagine that every person is like a helium balloon, and the helium inside the balloon represents each person's self-confidence. When you add helium, the balloon expands and floats upwards. Take helium out and it deflates, drops to the ground and shrinks.

My challenge for the week is to make it a HABIT to consciously "add helium" to people's balloons... Find ways to say or do something to others which increases the amount of helium – or self confidence – that they've got. Something that makes them feel good, feel special, feel appreciated. It could be a friend, employee, a client, family, your bank manager, the person at the check-out in Tesco – even the person who cuts in front of you in their car.

Why is this important?:

> Good will spreads. Think of the impact it could have in terms of increasing the sum of happiness and potential in the world if everyone adopted this attitude.
>
> It feels great to boost someone else's confidence.
>
> It makes you an extremely 'attractive' person.
>
> People will be drawn to you.
>
> Your own self-confidence will increase as a result.

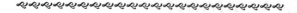

"A healthy male adult bore
consumes each year one and half
times his own weight in other
people's patience!"

John Updike

7. Energy Drainers

When I first set up my business I had a second-hand fax machine that didn't work properly. Almost every day something went wrong with it and every time it did I wasted valuable energy getting anxious and upset with it. In the end I gave up and bought a new one which works like a charm and I haven't wasted a nano-second of time worrying about it since.

Is there anything in your life that is draining your energy?

> A jacket that needs altering or cleaning
>
> Something in the house or garden that needs fixing
>
> Malfunctioning equipment
>
> A messy office
>
> A draining relationship
>
> An incomplete project
>
> A letter that needs writing

This week, pick at least three things (doesn't matter how small) that are draining YOUR energy and make a commitment to handle them once and for all. You'll feel so much better as a result.

Equally, just as things can drain energy, other things can actually boost our energy. What are these things for you? Taking a walk round in the park? Meditating? Listening to birdsong? Writing in a journal? Listening to some favourite music? Going out for a meal with a loved one?

Just as you choose to eliminate the things that are draining your energy, see if you can actively choose to ADD things to your life that give you positive energy.

"Come to the edge," he said.

They said, "We are afraid."

"Come to the edge," he said.

They came. He pushed them …

and they flew."

Guillaume Appollinaire

8. There's No Such Thing as a 'Wrong' Decision

For all those who have a hard time making decisions – this is for you:

In her excellent book, "Feel the Fear and Do It Anyway", Susan Jeffers points out that when we have a decision to make, we tend to look at it in terms of making either a 'right' choice or a 'wrong' choice. As a result, we find ourselves paralysed by being too scared of making the wrong decision.

Her suggestion is that we change our perspective and consider BOTH choices as being right. No matter what happens, whichever decision you make, it won't be wrong – it will simply result in a different outcome. Either way, there will be new things to learn, new people to meet, new opportunities will open up, and so on.

She calls it the 'No-Lose Model' and this perspective can really open one up to the possibilities of choices – rather than feeling restricted by them.

I know the feeling of being paralysed by indecision only too well. Several years ago I was absolutely incapable of making a decision as to whether or not to end a long-term relationship. Without the benefit of a crystal ball, I was so scared of making the 'wrong' decision that I literally couldn't move. In the end – five years later – I did make the choice to end the relationship, and within three months had met the wonderful man that I now share my life with.

The point is, that even if I hadn't experienced this admittedly fairy-tale ending, I know that lots of other opportunities would have come my way, and – as Jeffers emphasises – I WOULD have been able to deal with any of them.

"When we truly care for
ourselves it becomes possible to
care more profoundly about
other people."

Edith Le Shen

9. Go on, Spoil Yourself

For those of you who have seen the quirky TV series Twin Peaks (I confess to being a huge fan), this week's tip comes courtesy of Special Agent Cooper.

In one particular episode I noted an incident where he and the local police sheriff make an unscheduled stop in a busy day, in order to enjoy a cup of steaming black coffee. This despite the fact that they were in a hurry and didn't really have the time to do so. Cooper looks at the sheriff and says:

"Harry, I'm going to let you into a little secret. Every day, once a day – give yourself a present. Don't plan it – don't wait for it – just let it happen. It could be a new shirt from the men's store, a catnap in your office chair – or two cups of good hot black coffee."

What GREAT advice!

So, my challenge to you for this week is to start giving yourself a present each and every day. No matter how small. Something unexpected just for you.

"Take the first step in faith.
You don't have to see the whole staircase,
just take the first step."

Martin Luther King

10. Single Daily Action

If you are trying to reach a specific goal, or want to embark on a project but are having trouble getting started or motivated, a good strategy is to take action towards it on a daily basis.

No matter how small or simple this action is, some action is better than none, and soon you will start to gather momentum and begin to rocket towards reaching your target.

Some examples might be:

> Your goal is to write a novel or short story. You might choose to write just one paragraph or page a day.

> Your goal is to establish some new business connections with people in a particular field. You could make just two calls a day.

The most important thing is to GET INTO ACTION. Not only will you feel much more positive, you will soon start to see the results. Why not try this for the next week and see what happens.

What is/are your goal(s)?

What will your Single Daily Action(s) be?

Here's to an extraordinarily productive week!

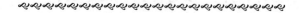

"If it doesn't absorb you,
if it isn't any fun, don't do it."

D.H. Lawrence

11. Beware the 'Shoulds'

How often do you use the word 'should'?

The things that we love to do – that are in line with who we are and our values – are never 'shoulds'. They are the things that we look forward to and which give us energy. 'Shoulds' are usually energy drainers (see Tip 7).

Whenever we say something like "I really should do ...." it implies that it's something that we don't really want to do – or that perhaps we feel someone else wants us to do. It also implies that we don't have a lot of choice in the matter.

Next time you catch yourself – or someone else – using the word 'should', try replacing it with 'COULD' instead. This immediately gives you the element of choice. It's not something you've got to do, it's something you can choose to do – or not. It's up to you.

Feels a lot better, doesn't it?

કહકહકહકહકહકહકહકહકહકહકહકહકહ

"If you never say 'no' then what
is your 'yes' worth?"

(Anon)

કહકહકહકહકહકહકહકહકહકહકહકહ

12. Just Say 'NO!'

IN ALL MY YEARS AS A COACH, ONE OF THE MOST PERSISTENT ISSUES MY CLIENTS HAVE BROUGHT TO THE TABLE IS NEEDING TO SAY 'NO' MORE OFTEN.

It doesn't matter whether you're talking about business or personal situations, it is crucial to be able to say 'no' to those things that don't serve you. For example, volunteering to serve on a committee which is going to take you away from your family for yet another evening in the month; being inveigled into organising the PTA Summer Fair which takes up all the spare time you would have preferred to spend writing or gardening; spending a day with a 'friend' who does nothing but complain and drain your energy.

Many of us find it really difficult to say 'no'. There are lots of reasons: Perhaps we're flattered to be asked; to say 'no' means you're not a team player; maybe we don't want to let people down – or to appear to be rude or selfish, or we simply like being liked! Just remember that EVERY TIME YOU SAY 'YES' YOU ARE EFFECTIVELY SAYING 'NO' TO SOMETHING ELSE. And that 'something else' may be something which is really important to you.

Here's a way to measure the relative merits of those claims on your time when you're trying to decide whether to say 'yes' or 'no' to something:

By saying YES to: I am saying NO to:

1. _____   _____

2. _____   _____

3. _____   _____

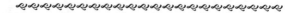

"Man's mind stretched to a new
idea never goes back to its
original shape."

Oliver Wendell Holmes

13. Brainstorming

Brainstorm: A spontaneous group discussion to produce ideas and ways of solving problems. *(New Oxford Dictionary of English)*

I love brainstorming! Let's say you are facing a particular challenge, or you have the seeds of an idea in your head or you want to generate lots of ideas and strategies. Rather than sitting in splendid isolation with a pen and piece of paper, it can be infinitely more productive (and more enjoyable) to gather several friends and /or colleagues and brainstorm together.

Elect a note taker – or turn on a tape recorder so that no ideas or comments are lost. Ask people to think out of the box – and NEVER discard an idea, even if at first it seems totally impracticable.

Once you've got a list of ideas and suggestions, take each one in turn – even the most 'off the wall' ones – and ask these four questions:

1. What is the useful element in this idea?
2. What are the problematic aspects of this idea?
3. How can I get around the impractical elements of this idea?
4. What further ideas does this idea inspire?

The key point here is that even though an idea might seem fraught with difficulties, don't discard it. It's quite possible that – on closer examination – another workable idea can come from it.

"We all live in suspense, from day
to day, from hour to hour; in
other words, we are the hero of
our own story."

Mary McCarthy

14. Time Wasters

We all have the same 24 hours in a day, but sometimes it just doesn't feel like enough time. There's often more to do than we can possibly manage in the time available. So we need to make wise choices about how we apportion that time and energy.

Think for a moment about the 80/20 Rule. That is, 20% of all our activities are likely to produce 80% of the meaningful results in our lives.

With this in mind, try to identify your Top Three Time Wasters – in other words, stuff that you spend too much time doing and which produces minimal results.

When you've done this, decide what you will do to eliminate them – and put it into practice TODAY. As an example:

Time Waster: Spending far too long on emails.

Solution: Only check emails twice a day max.

To take this further, you might also like to identify your Top Three Time Maximisers. These are the activities that are really worthwhile to you, be it in terms of financial gain or perhaps time that you take for creativity, your family, for exercise or spiritual and intellectual growth.

What can you do to ensure that you are giving these priority?

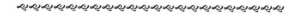

"Sometimes with secret pride I sigh
to think how tolerant am I:
then wonder which is really mine
tolerance, or a rubber spine?"

Ogden Nash

15. Defining Boundaries

I recently spotted a sign at the entrance to a building site. Clearly intended for those working on the site, its message couldn't have been simpler:

NO HAT

NO BOOTS

NO JOB!

I found myself thinking, if only we could be as clear, concise and straightforward in our approach to relationships how much easier things would be. As a general rule, we seem to find it hard to state clearly what our needs are, and more specifically, what behaviour we consider to be acceptable from others and what behaviour isn't. So often, we skirt around the issue, dropping hints here and there and hoping that the other person will catch on.

Establishing strong boundaries around what is and isn't acceptable from others is extremely important for successful, healthy relationships. Boundaries are like an imaginary line of protection that you draw around you. Examples of people overstepping your boundaries might be: your spouse criticising you in front of others; unthinking friends who call you late at night when you're getting ready for bed; a co-worker who makes a habit of shedding their workload onto you.

So what can we do about this? The first step is to become clear in your own mind about what behaviour is acceptable to you and what isn't. Then you will need to communicate this to those around you.

This needn't be done in an angry or proscriptive way. All you are doing, in effect, is making clear to others that you respect yourself and you ask that they respect you, too.

Pro rata, you could invite them to let you know if there are any ways in which you are overstepping their boundaries – and take steps to modify your behaviour accordingly.

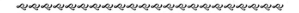

"The key is not to
prioritise your schedule,
but to schedule your priorities."

Stephen Covey

16. Rocks, Gravel and Sand

In his book "First Things First" Stephen Covey describes a lecture he attended on the topic of 'time'. The lecturer took a large glass jar and set it down on a table with some small rocks beside it. He placed the rocks in the jar and asked the audience whether they thought the jar was full.

Everybody laughed and replied that yes, it was full. Then the lecturer reached under the table and pulled out a container of gravel. He poured in the gravel and shook the jar so that the gravel filled the spaces that had been left by the rocks. Again he asked the audience if the jar was full. By this time they had cottoned on, and replied no.

'Good!' he replied. And he reached under the table and repeated the process, only this time with sand, which went into the spaces left by the rocks and the gravel. Then he asked what had been the point of the demonstration.

Somebody said, 'Well, there are gaps, and if you really work at it, you can always fit more into your life.'

'No,' he said, 'that's not the point. The point is this: if you hadn't put these big rocks in first, would you ever have gotten any of them in?'

If we relate this illustration to our lives, the 'rocks' are representative of the things that are really important to us. The gravel represents the other things in life that matter, but on a smaller scale. The sand is everything else. The small stuff. If we put the sand and gravel into the jar first, there's no room for the rocks.

As Covey says, take care of the rocks first – the things that really matter. Set your priorities. The rest is just gravel and sand.

"The secret of getting ahead is getting started.

The secret of getting started is breaking your complex, overwhelming tasks into small manageable tasks and then starting on the first one."

Mark Twain

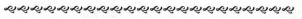

17. Procrastination

Over the years I've come across some really cracking examples of procrastination. Recently, my sister told me about a friend of hers – an eminent academic – who confessed she'd chosen to remove the accumulated grease from the back of her cooker with a teaspoon rather than start work on an article for an academic journal.

A colleague of mine finally finished reading "The Procrastinator's Handbook", having admitted taking it back to the library three times to renew it!

For those of us for whom these examples sound all too familiar, here are a few tips to help beat the demon of procrastination:

1. Ask yourself: "If this task is something I keep putting off, is it something I need to do at all? Can I shelve it completely? Is it no longer relevant to my life? Could I delegate it?" If not, just do it.

2. Sometimes a task can seem so immense and overwhelming that it literally paralyses us. Break the task down and ask yourself "what's the one thing I need to do to get started?" It may be to turn the computer on; write the first sentence; make the first call. Whatever it is, just do it.

3. Give yourself a short time limit to work on the task. Time Management Coach, Mark Forster, suggests setting a kitchen timer for, say, 10-15 minutes and ONLY working on the task for that amount of time. You'll be amazed at how well this technique works.

4. Do it first. Whatever you're putting off, do it first otherwise it will slip to the bottom of the list and most probably stay there to be superseded by other, less important tasks.

"You don't get to choose
how you're going to die,
or when.
You can only decide
how you're going to live. Now."

Joan Baez

18. Where There's a Will, There's a Way

Just recently I have heard some dreadful stories from people who are trying to sort out a loved one's estate in the absence of a will.

I know it's not the sort of thing that anybody wants to think about, but if you die without leaving a will it can be an absolute nightmare for those you leave behind.

This may seem an unlikely subject for an inspiring Coaching Tip, but through discussions with clients and with friends I know that the mere fact of NOT having made – or updated – your will can be a huge energy drainer. It's something that we all know we need to do – something that we put off – and consequently it drains our energy whenever we allow ourselves to think about it.

Have YOU made – or recently updated – your will?

If not, I challenge you to stop procrastinating and get it done. This week.

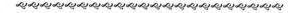

"Life's most urgent question is,
'What are you doing for others?'"

Martin Luther King

19. Something Special

A friend recently told me a great story. Her husband called her from work and told her that he had devised a very special treat, but that she could only have it if she guessed what it was. Intrigued, she called him back several times trying to guess, and a tantalising 'twenty questions' ensued. Eventually she guessed what the treat was – he had gone to great lengths to secure two tickets for a concert that she really wanted to go to as a special treat.

This story impressed me on two levels: firstly, for those of us with a well-developed Romance Gene – how romantic is that??!!!

And secondly, I know how easy it is to take those close to you for granted – and how important it is every now and again to take the time, thought and trouble to do something special for them.

Is there anyone in your life that you want to do something special for this week?

Is there anyone you need to say 'thank you' to?

Is there someone who needs to know how much they mean to you?

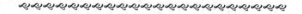

"The man least dependant upon
the morrow goes to meet the
morrow most cheerfully."

Epicurus

20. What's Your Theme?

Every now and again I will ask my clients to identify a 'theme' for themselves – something they would like to focus their attention on in the weeks to come.

The key is to choose a theme that will inspire you to think more positively about something – or help you to focus on changes you would like to make.

Here are some real examples of themes that people have chosen:

"Put myself first"

"If it isn't fun, don't do it!""

"Look smart"

"Delegate, delegate, delegate"

"Leave early for all appointments"

"Live in the moment"

What would you like your theme to be for the next week?

Choose something that you'd like to focus on in the next seven days that will really make a difference to your life. Write your theme on post-its and scatter them strategically around your home or office – where you will notice them frequently.

When our heads are all too often crammed with mental 'to do' lists, this exercise can really help to act as a conscious reminder to focus on something positive.

"Every man must be his own leader.

He now knows enough not to follow other people. He must follow the light that's within himself and through this light he will create a new community."

Laurens Van Der Post

21. The Soldier and the Priest

"I once heard this story about a priest, who was confronted by a soldier while he was walking down a road in pre-revolutionary Russia. The soldier, aiming his rifle at the priest, commanded, 'Who are you? Where are you going? Why are you going there?'

Unfazed, the priest calmly replied, 'How much do they pay you?'

Somewhat surprised, the soldier responded, 'Twenty-five kopecks a month.'

The priest paused, and in a deeply thoughtful manner said, 'I have a proposal for you. I'll pay you fifty kopecks each month if you stop me here every day and challenge me to respond to those same three questions.'"

(Taken from *Leadership From the Inside Out* by Kevin Cashman)

꣠꣠꣠꣠꣠꣠꣠꣠꣠꣠꣠꣠꣠꣠꣠꣠꣠꣠꣠꣠꣠

This is such a good story. The questions seem simple enough, but of course, they require considerable thought and a deep examination of your future direction.

How would YOU respond to those same three questions?

Who are you?

Where are you going?

Why are you going there?

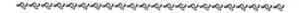

"May I treat others as I would be treated. What I like not for myself may I dispense not to others."

A Sufi prayer

22. Verbal Paper Cuts

Paper cuts are those irritating, superficial cuts that you can get from mishandling paper. Little blood is lost, but they can be painful for several days.

The paper cut is a useful metaphor for relationships. Has anyone ever made a 'cutting' comment to you that seemed superficial on the surface, but that caused you considerable discomfort? Have YOU ever said unkind words to someone else? Your intent was probably not to hurt them – but the result of unkind words, even if spoken in jest, can be like the sting of a paper cut.

If you'd like to get rid of 'verbal paper cuts' in a relationship here are a few suggestions:

1. Firstly, just become aware of what it feels like to give or receive a verbal paper cut.

2. Ask those close to you to give you honest feedback. Make a clear agreement with those close to you to let you know when you've made a hurtful remark. Agree that you'll do the same if they say something hurtful to you.

3. When a 'verbal paper cut' is made by anyone, ask the questions, "What was the reason I said those things? Is there some unspoken resentment there that I haven't dealt with? Was I being funny at someone else's expense?"

4. Finally, take steps to deal with the anger or resentment in a conscious and constructive fashion.

(Based on an article by Bernice Ross and Byron Van Arsdale)

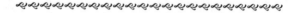

"The ability to simplify means
to eliminate the unnecessary
so that the necessary may speak."

Hans Hofmann

23. Keep It Simple

One of the contradictions of modern life is that despite the introduction of labour-saving devices and the burgeoning of Information Technology – we all seem to be increasingly busy, rushed and overburdened.

One way to combat this problem is to SIMPLIFY the way we live and work. As an example, I am frequently asked for directions to my office. I used to type out the directions every time which was, of course, ludicrously time consuming. I now have templates for directions to my office from all directions. Just taking the steps to put this simple system in place has already saved me lots of time.

What steps could you take to simplify your life? Here are a handful of ideas to start you thinking:

Create a series of standard business letters so that you don't have to create new ones from scratch every time.

Set up standing orders or direct debits so that bills are paid automatically. This way you don't have to worry about them, or take the time to write cheques and post them off.

Shop only once a week – even better, order online and have your groceries delivered to your door.

Set up a reminder system for birthdays, anniversaries, or important events. You can buy a selection of birthday cards at one time rather than having to buy them individually each time.

Look at all your commitments and ask yourself which ones are no longer necessary or are not genuinely serving your life. Then consider how you could simply drop them, phase them out or delegate them.

Keep your life simple – and have a great week!

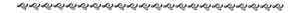

"The world of ours has been
constructed like a superbly
written novel; we pursue the tale
with avidity, hoping to discover
the plot."

Sir Arthur Keith

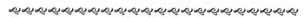

24. Manageable Goals

Sometimes a goal can seem so overwhelming that you just don't know where to start. And that's a sure-fire excuse to put it off!

In her book, "Wishcraft – How to Get What You Really Want", Barbara Sher suggests that you start from the end and work backwards – breaking the goal down into smaller and smaller action steps. The key is to keep asking yourself two questions:

1. Can I do this tomorrow? (and if the answer is no ...)
2. What would I have to get done first?

I used this process to work through a goal of mine which is to have a book published in the next 12 months.

Can I do this tomorrow? *If only it was that simple!*

What would I have to get done first? *Well, I'd need to write the book, obviously.*

Can I do this tomorrow? *Absolutely not.*

What would I have to get done first? *I'd need to do some research and then start writing at least a couple of pages a day.*

By following this process my action steps – working from the end – now look something like this:

> Get book published
> Find publisher/research self-publishing
> Write book
> Research
> Write at least 2 pages a day
> Draft outline and chapters
> Go to library, start reading around the subject.

These are things that I could start doing today. Even with less ambitious goals the process works just as well, and can do wonders to break the cycle of procrastination and get you started.

∾∾∾∾∾∾∾∾∾∾∾∾∾∾∾∾∾∾∾∾∾∾∾

"Change your thoughts and you
change your world."

Norman Vincent Peale

∾∾∾∾∾∾∾∾∾∾∾∾∾∾∾∾∾∾∾∾∾∾∾

25. Awareness

"Awareness is the precursor of change."

"Awareness is the precursor of CHOICE."

These are two of my favourite sayings. In the process of self-development and personal change, becoming aware of what's not working is the first crucial step.

Once you've identified that, it's then up to you to CHOOSE whether to keep things the way they are, or to take the steps to change them.

If you choose to change, then part of the process is to increase your awareness. Let's say you've decided to stop being critical – either of yourself or of others.

1. Simply start to notice each and every time you do this.

2. Count the number of times in a day or a week you do it.

3. Keep a written log if it helps you to keep focused.

As you increase your awareness, you'll automatically begin to check yourself and eventually you'll find that you've stopped altogether.

"Yesterday is not ours to recover,
but tomorrow is ours to win or lose."

Lyndon B Johnson

26. Reflections

It's hard to believe that we're more than half way through the year. With summer upon us, and many people getting ready to go on holiday, this is a great time to reflect on what you have achieved in the first half of the year, and also how you would like the next five months to look.

Step One:

Think about all of your achievements so far this year – note them all, either in your mind or on paper. Make it as long a list as you can and then give yourself a real or imaginary pat on the back for everything – no matter how small – that you have achieved.

Step Two:

Consider the rest of the year. How would you like your life to be different by the end of this year? Another way to look at this is to project yourself forward to December 31st and look back over the last 5 months. What would have to have happened for you to feel thoroughly contented with the way this year has progressed?

Step Three:

Make a list of three key things that you would like to achieve by the end of the year. Is there a new and different challenge you'd like to set yourself? Is there something you've been wanting to do for ages, but you keep putting it off? Why not include something outrageous or unexpected on your list?

"Life is not the way it's supposed
to be. It's the way it is. The way
you cope with it is what makes
the difference."

Virginia Satir

27. Clearing the Decks

Have you ever been in a situation where you've taken so much on that you feel completely swamped and don't know where to start?

If this feels familiar, here's a tip that might help you to take back control:

1. Make a list of ALL the things you're currently doing – all the activities, projects, hobbies etc.

2. Mentally 'clear the decks' – in other words, assume that you no longer have to do any of these things. Your diary is totally empty – your time is 100% your own.

3. Then CHOOSE those activities that you want to put back on the list. Think very carefully. Be ruthless. Be highly selective.

Be sure that you only put back those activities that you feel genuinely enthusiastic about. Examine carefully those things you think you *should* or *ought* to do.

There may be some things you feel you have to put back, but wish you didn't. Listen carefully to that and ask yourself: "Are these activities ones that I might want to drop or to delegate?"

Clearing the Decks is a great way to eliminate 'shoulds' and to help you make conscious choices about how you want to spend your precious time.

ᗣᗣᗣᗣᗣᗣᗣᗣᗣᗣᗣᗣᗣᗣᗣᗣᗣᗣᗣᗣᗣᗣ

"Trifles make perfection,

but perfection is no trifle."

(Italian proverb)

ᗣᗣᗣᗣᗣᗣᗣᗣᗣᗣᗣᗣᗣᗣᗣᗣᗣᗣᗣᗣᗣᗣ

28. Your Perfect Day

Do you remember that wonderful Lou Reed song 'Perfect Day'? It was the song that the BBC used some time ago to accompany their advertising campaign. I heard it again the other day and it got me thinking about the concept of creating a perfect day – what it would contain, what you would be doing, who you would share it with, how it would feel...

What would YOUR perfect day look like?

Why not sit down and write a description of your perfect day. If you write it in the present tense as if it's actually happening – it will make it more real. Remember – there's no right or wrong to this – everyone's concept of 'perfect' is going to be completely unique. If the idea grabs you, you can really be creative with this – give yourself permission to dream.

Once you've done this, ask yourself what steps you are willing to take to incorporate at least some elements of your perfect day into your life on a regular basis?

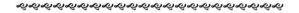

"Your own resolution to succeed
is more important than any
other one thing."

Abraham Lincoln

29. Success

I recently had a fascinating discussion with a colleague where we were talking about our definitions of 'Success.' Even though we work in the same field and have much in common, it struck me how radically our personal definitions varied.

Of course, everyone's definition of success is going to be different. For some success might be measured in terms of wealth and material possessions – for others it could be related to personal relationships – for others, perhaps reaching a particular level in their work or business would be all-important. More realistically, it is probably a combination of many things.

Ironically, there are those who seem to have all the external 'trappings of success' – lots of money, great job, 'happy' family – but inside they are absolutely miserable. Their seemingly happy life is totally incongruent with who they are and what's really important to them.

What's YOUR definition of success?

Knowing what success really means to you makes it much easier to act with certainty in life, and to create a life that will be fulfilling. It also makes things a lot easier when you are faced with decisions about your future.

"Everything changes
when you change."

Jim Rohn

30. Tolerations

What are you 'tolerating' in your life? In other words, what are you putting up with? And how much is that draining your energy?

'Tolerations' are those things that irritate and frustrate you – they make you sigh each time you think of them – your heart sinks and you can almost feel the energy being sapped from you. You know you need to sort them out, but somehow they keep being dropped to the bottom of the 'to do' list. Tolerations could be:

    the button that needs sewing onto your favourite shirt
    filthy car
    cluttered desk
    broken microwave
    front door that needs painting
    overdue letter or conversation

They may seem insignificant, but even the smallest things can build up to the point where they have an adverse impact on our energy levels. So it's important to become aware of 'tolerations' and eliminate them on a regular basis. Here's how to do it:

Step One:
Make a list of everything in your life that you're currently tolerating – big and small.

Step Two:
Pick FIVE and handle them in the next week – just get rid of them – in whatever way you choose.

Step Three:
Keep working through the list until all the items have been eliminated. It will make a huge difference, and will free up lots of energy for more positive pursuits.

Step Four:
Repeat this exercise every 3-4 months.

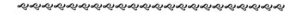

"If the only prayer you say in
your whole life is 'thank you'
that would suffice."

Meister Eckhart

31. Gratitude

At certain times – particularly when life is throwing a series of ugly challenges at you – it can be very easy to dwell on all the problems, difficulties and negatives and to forget – or take for granted – those aspects of our lives which are working well for us.

Here are a couple of tips to keep you focused on the positives:

1. Make a list of at least 20 things you currently feel thankful for. This may take some thought, but if you persist you'll be surprised at what you can come up with. If certain people appear on your list you may want to let them know.

2. A Daily "Gratitude Journal": Some people find it inspiring to sit down at the end of each day and write down all the things they are feeling grateful for.

3. When author Jinny Ditzler (author of "Your Best Year Yet") and her husband were going through a rough time, they used to get together one night a week, open a bottle of wine and take turns making toasts for the best things that had happened the previous week. She writes: "even in the worst weeks, there are those little miracles and things to be grateful for. It makes such a difference to remember to focus on how lucky we are rather than on what a struggle it all is."

You'll be surprised at the impact 'focusing on the positives' can have to your attitude and sense of well-being.

"Only dull people are
brilliant at breakfast!"

Oscar Wilde

32. Natural Energy Cycles

We all have different 'natural energy cycles' – in other words, times of the day when our energy is naturally high or low.

I'm a 'morning' person, whereas I know people who do their best creative work burning the midnight oil. I've learned to recognise now when my energy is low and I consciously use those times for activities that don't require a lot of physical or mental effort.

When are you at your best? What times of day do you feel bright, clear-headed, full of energy? And when do you typically feel sluggish, fuzzy, tired?

Start to recognise these times and consciously use the times when you have most energy for those tasks that require more mental effort. The 'down' times are best utilised for more routine activities.

This is often easier said than done, but once you become more aware of this you can try to match the different tasks to the available energy levels, and build these in as part of your routine.

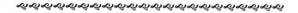

"Much unhappiness has come
into the world because of
bewilderment and things
left unsaid."

Dostoevsky

33. When in Doubt, Communicate!

Are you afraid to communicate what you really feel for fear of making waves, or hurting someone else? Sometimes it feels 'easier' not to say anything at all rather than face a potentially difficult discussion. The problem then, of course, is that the longer things go unsaid, the greater the likelihood of misunderstanding.

A couple of weeks ago I read an article about the band REM who broke up because – in the words of one of the members – they had become 'hopelessly estranged and terminally uncommunicative.' They saw no solution to the problem and the band dissolved.

However, eventually they pulled themselves around and determined to get back together. How did they do it? To quote Michael Stipe, the lead singer, "We talked. We just sat down and talked."

This sounds ludicrously simple – but it really can be just that simple. Communication can almost always resolve a problem. It just takes determination on everyone's part to sort it out and a total commitment to speak the truth. Here are a few tips:

1. Make it very safe for each person to communicate what needs to be said. Even though what the other person is saying may be hard for you to hear, don't get defensive and leap down their throat.

2. Listen and try to hear each other's point of view, and to understand it as they see it, rather than filtering it through your own experience. You may not agree with it, but it IS real for them.

3. Be sure to acknowledge what the other person has said even though you may not agree with it. Feeling heard is vital. Just a comment like "I can understand that" or "I see what you mean" is all it takes for the other person to feel heard and understood.

"How many people on their
deathbed wish they'd spent
more time at the office?"

Stephen Covey

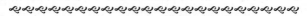

34. Priorities

Sometimes we can get so caught up in the whirlpool of day-to-day living that we lose sight of those things we truly love to do; those things that are intrinsically 'us', that we feel passionate about, that make us naturally happy – content – excited – full of energy.

To re-connect with what some of these things might be, get yourself a pen and a piece of paper and then ask yourself this question:

"If money were not a consideration, how would I choose to spend my time?"

Write down the first ten things that come to mind...

How many of these things are you doing on a regular basis?

Clearly, I'm not suggesting that making a living is not important – or that you give up your work. What I AM suggesting is that if you feel you've lost sight of what you really love to do – then perhaps some re-prioritising might be in order.

What will you have to do differently in order to make room for some or all of the things on your list?

"Though we travel the world
over to find the beautiful,
we must carry it within us, or we
find it not."

Ralph Waldo Emerson

35. Feel Good Folder

Even the most positive among us can get the blues from time to time. There are those times when everything seems to be against us; nothing is working the way we want; or when someone says or does something that knocks our confidence.

Over the years, I've learned a great technique to counter these 'down' times, and that is to actively collect things that boost your confidence and make you feel good. It might be a positive, loving or encouraging letter that someone has sent you – or a card or email. Even a postcard or reminder of a time when you were feeling on top of the world.

Put these reminders into a box or file or drawer (or perhaps keep them in a special folder on the computer) and whenever you're feeling a bit down, simply reach for the file and read the contents. I call mine my 'Feel Good Folder' and it sits by the side of my desk.

It's remarkable how easy it is to forget all the positives – especially when you're feeling a bit negative – and these reminders will go a long way towards restoring your confidence and sense of well-being.

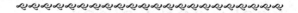

"Invent your world. Surround
yourself with people, colour,
sounds and work that
nourish you."

Sark

36. Success Teams

Whatever you want to achieve in your life – either on a personal or professional level – there's nothing like having a positive support team behind you, encouraging you at every turn; keeping you on track and picking you up and dusting you off again when you stumble along the way.

Equally, if there are people in your life who are consistently eating away at your self-confidence, it can have the opposite effect and tip the scales towards your no longer believing that you can achieve the goals you have set yourself.

You'd be surprised how negative people come out of the woodwork when you announce that you are actively seeking to make positive changes in your life – and will do all they can to hold you back.

Think about the people in your life. Do they support you 100% and provide constructive advice and feedback? Will they cheer you on to win? Will they celebrate your successes and encourage you when you encounter setbacks?

Who will you choose to have on your own personal Success Team?

Who do you know who could help YOU to achieve your goals? Why not start your own Success Team today with a handful of supportive friends or colleagues.

"What is without
periods of rest
will not endure."

Ovid

37. Take a Break!

You've been sitting for several minutes staring blankly at the same page of a book, the same computer screen, or a particular piece of work, but you don't seem to be able to concentrate or make any progress? Sound familiar?

When you find that your focus is dwindling this is your body giving you a big hint that it's time to take a break. Here are some tips for making any break you take more effective:

The best type of breaks entail not only changing the type of activity you're doing, but also your location. So, if you've been working at the computer in your office, it might be beneficial to get up and make yourself a cup of tea or, if feasible, take a walk round the block.

Avoid confusing 'diversions' with 'breaks'. For example, if you're working on the computer and you take a 'break' by playing computer games, you've only created a diversion, not a true break. Remember, an effective break requires a change of both location and activity.

Move your body! Exercise promotes the circulation, which increases the amount of oxygen in the brain – this helps to keep you alert and thinking clearly.

Get outside for some fresh air – and hopefully some sunshine. This is a great way to relax your mind and clear your thoughts.

Programme periodic breaks in your schedule throughout the day. Planning breaks in advance helps you to create a rhythm and balance to your schedule as well as keeping you refreshed.

(Taken from *The Art of Taking a Break* by Bernice Ross & Byron Van Arsdale)

"Your happiness depends on
three things, all of which are
within your power;

your will,

your ideas concerning the events
in which you are involved,

and the use you make
of your ideas."

Epicetus

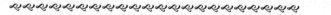

38. Capture Your Ideas

Ideas are precious. They are to be kept, treasured and nurtured.

You know how it is. You have a fantastic idea, but you're rushing somewhere, or you're simply too busy and you don't get a chance to write it down and then it vanishes like a dream at the moment of waking.

As a writer, I have, for many years, adopted the habit of having a small notebook which I carry everywhere with me. You just never know when you'll overhear a snippet of a conversation or see a drama unfold before you which might come in handy for a story at some point in the future.

So here's your tip for this week. Buy yourself a book where you can store each and every idea you think of. It will need to be instantly accessible, yet small enough to carry around with you. Maybe you'll have two – one for the home or office and one for when you're out and about. I've been told – though I don't know if it's true – that Richard Branson has eight!

The thing about ideas is that even if they seem irrelevant or impossible at the time, they may very well leap into relevance months or even years later.

Capture your ideas. Don't let them float away. You never know when you might need them.

"Maintaining a complicated life is
a great way to avoid changing it."

Elaine St. James

39. What Are You Avoiding?

Is your life excessively busy? Do you feel as if you wake up in the morning and step straight onto the hamster wheel, be it at home or at work? Are you always rushing around and constantly trying to catch up? Is your life unnecessarily complicated?

Making ourselves BUSY can be the most wonderfully clever strategy for avoiding something that really needs attention in our lives. If this sounds as if it might be true for you, then ask yourself: "Is there something important that I'm effectively avoiding?"

Give yourself time to think about this – it may not be an easy admission to make.

This issue cropped up for me last year, and I have been consciously carving out time for myself to concentrate on the questions that surfaced as a result. These were not questions that could be easily answered – no wonder I had managed to avoid them so successfully for so long by making myself so 'busy'!!!

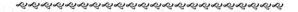

When one door closes another
one opens; but we often look so
long and regretfully upon the
closed door, that we do not see
the ones which open for us."

Helen Keller

40. Opening Doors

There was a scene in the Beatles film "Yellow Submarine" where John Lennon finds himself in an endless corridor with lots of doors on either side. Each door opens onto a completely different scenario and he tries each one before deciding which scene he wants to step into.

I often think of this when there's a decision to be made. It can sometimes help to literally imagine opening a door and looking at what's on the other side. Select a different door for all the options you're considering, open each one and see what it looks like on the other side. If you don't like what you see, close the door and forget that option. If it looks enticing, try stepping through the door and see what it feels like.

To take this one step further, you can choose a specific length of time – anywhere from 5 minutes to several hours or days – and 'act as if' you had decided to pursue that particular course for that length of time. 'Trying on' a decision to see how it fits can make it more real and give you a taste of how it would be to actually live with it.

If it doesn't feel right, don't forget that you can always step back into the corridor and close the door behind you.

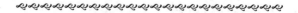

"And the day came when the risk
it took to remain tight in a bud
was more painful than the risk it
took to blossom."

Anaïs Nin

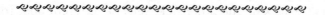

41. Comfort Zones

At the beginning of this year, I decided that one of my goals was going to be to do more public speaking. Since then I have given talks to audiences ranging in size from 20 to 200 people.

Talking in front of an audience is way outside my comfort zone. In fact, a year ago you couldn't have paid me a small fortune to do it. I definitely fell into that surprisingly large category of people who would "rather die than speak in front of an audience."

Several months ago, while driving home from my first talk, I can remember grinning from ear to ear and quite literally feeling 'bigger' as a person.

Pushing the limits of your personal comfort zone is really challenging, but the effects are hugely rewarding. It expands your horizons, boosts your confidence and helps you to feel that you can take on ever bigger and better things.

What will YOU do this week to step out of your comfort zone? It doesn't matter how small that step is, by daring to take it you will 'grow' and so will your confidence.

"Success is knowing that if today
were your last day on earth you
could leave without regret."

Sarah Ban Breathnach

42. Completions

This week's Tip comes from a very personal experience. Recently I learned that my ex-mother-in-law had died. I was very fond of her, and had always felt sad that the break up of my marriage had resulted in my estrangement from her and my father-in-law.

Every now and again over the years I would think to myself that I really must make the effort to go to London and pop in and see them. I knew that they held no animosity towards me and it would have been really good to repair any misunderstandings that might have taken place, and restore what had once been a close relationship.

I never did it. Now, of course, it's too late and I regret that I never made the time.

Is there anyone in your life that you would dearly like to have such a meeting – or such a conversation with?

What do you need to say?

If there are any 'incomplete' situations in your life, why not make the effort to do whatever you have to do to feel 'complete' once more? It may not feel very comfortable, but you'll be very glad that you did.

"He who possesses most must be
most afraid of loss."

Leonardo Da Vinci

43. Decluttering

There's nothing like a really good clear out to make you feel great and to literally and metaphorically 'clear some space' in your life.

If your home or office needs a visit from the Decluttering Police, here are a few tips to help you to be ruthless about those items you are finding it hard to make a decision about.

Paper Mountain: It can be really hard to throw pieces of paper away – especially when the phrase "but I might need to refer to it later" keeps playing in your head. The most useful tip I've come across is to ask yourself – If I did need this in the future, is there some way that I could get hold of it again? In other words, could you ask the person who sent it to you to send you another copy? Could you download the information from the internet? Could you somehow reproduce the information in another way? If the answer is 'yes' it's a lot easier to make the decision to throw it away.

Clothing, books and other items: If you're finding it difficult to throw or give something away, try this trick. Get a bin liner, put the items into it, tie it up, put the date on the outside and store it somewhere like the garage or a shed. If you haven't needed any of the items within twelve months, throw the bag away (or give it to charity) – WITHOUT LOOKING INSIDE!

Ask for help: If you're still short on will power, choose a friend or colleague who you know to be decisive and ask them to help you. It's much easier for an outsider to be ruthless.

Hold a Decluttering Party: Make it fun! Send out for some pizza, and invite some friends round to help you decide which things to keep or which to get rid of. You never know, they might even want to take some of the items off your hands for you!

"Slow down and enjoy life. It's
not only the scenery you miss by
going too fast – you also miss the
sense of where you're going and
why."

Eddie Cantor

44. Busy vs. Productive

One of the most common complaints I hear from people is that they are just 'too busy'. There's too much to do and not enough hours in the day to do it in.

There's a very clear distinction between being 'busy' and being 'productive'. In some cases we make ourselves busy in order to avoid doing those things that may be more demanding, but really important.

Over the next week, notice when you are busy and ask yourself: Are the things you are doing truly productive? Could you actually delegate some of those tasks, or even drop them altogether? Are you caught up in Time Wasters? If so, be ruthless about dropping those activities and concentrate instead on things that are really going to produce a result.

Extra Tip!

How about coming up with an instant scoring system? Give yourself a mark out of ten on each of the things you find yourself doing throughout the day. If you can't give it more than a '5' then think seriously about not doing it and moving on to something more productive.

"When I stand before God at the
end of my life, I would hope that
I would not have a single talent
left, and could say, 'I used
everything you gave me.'"

Erma Bombeck

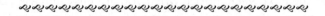

45. I Would Pick More Daisies

This week's Tip is taken from "The Procrastinator's Handbook" by Rita Emmett, and is written by Nadine Stair of Louisville, Kentucky. Nadine Stair was 85 years old when she wrote this:

"I'd dare to make more mistakes next time. I'd relax. I would limber up. I would be sillier than I have been this trip. I would take fewer things seriously. I would take more chances. I would take more trips. I would climb more mountains and swim more rivers. I would eat more ice cream and less beans. I would per- haps have more actual troubles, but I'd have fewer imaginary ones.

You see, I'm one of those people who live sensibly and sanely hour after hour, day after day. Oh, I've had my moments, and if I had it to do over again, I'd have more of them. In fact, I'd try to have nothing else. Just moments. One after another, instead of living so many years ahead of each day.

I've been one of those people who never go anywhere without a thermometer, a hot water bottle, a raincoat and a parachute. If I had it to do again, I would travel lighter next time.

If I had my life to live over, I would start barefoot earlier in the spring and stay that way later in the autumn. I would go to more dances. I would ride more merry-go-rounds. I would pick more daisies."

"Abundance is not something we acquire.
It is something we tune into."

Wayne Dyer

46. Creating Reserves

When I first started in business I had an inkjet printer which consumed ink cartridges at an alarming rate. Because they were so expensive, I tended to buy them one at a time, but in the back of my mind was a constant nagging worry that at any minute the ink would run out and I'd be left high and dry.

Eventually I decided that I was expending far too much energy worrying about this, so I bit the bullet and bought a stack of them to have in reserve. It's incredible the difference this made – no longer worrying if I was about to run out – no longer having 'just enough' but instead creating a safety cushion for myself.

The idea behind creating reserves is that you always have 'more than enough' rather than teetering on the brink of having 'only just enough'. Not wasting valuable energy worrying about not having enough can be immensely liberating – you will feel significantly calmer and more in control, and you will be working from a position of strength rather than a position of need.

Here are some other examples:

Always have ample petrol in your tank

Make sure you have sufficient money available for unexpected emergency expenditures

Leave early for appointments so that you never have to rush or panic about being late

Get lots of sleep so that you have reserves of energy

Book social events into the diary on a regular basis to be sure that you have a sufficient reserve of FUN!

Where do YOU need to create reserves?

"The communicating of a man's
self to his friend works two
contrary effects: for it
redoubleth joys and cutteth
griefs in half."

Francis Bacon

47. Mutual Support

This week's tip is mostly relevant to those of you who are married or living with partners – but it could be equally useful to anyone who shares a house or office with others.

One of the most reassuring things in life is to know that you have all the support you need – and also that you are able to provide support for others in the same way.

Every Sunday evening my partner Don and I get together with our diaries and discuss the coming week. We look at the dates when either one of us is particularly busy and likely to feel under pressure. If possible the other will be there to take the strain and cook dinner or provide any extra support that's needed. If we're both busy, then maybe we'll decide to go out to dinner that evening. At the very least, we both know what the other is doing and so misunderstandings or crossed appointments are less likely.

The key is that we approach the exercise from the standpoint of "how can I best support you this week?"

OK, you don't have to do the diaries bit, but it does work really well! So the tip for this week is to ask your loved ones – or your business colleagues – or your children, "how can I best support you this week?"

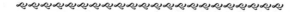

"The path to financial freedom
can be long and challenging.
The commitment to become
responsible with money is the
key that opens the flood gates
to more."

Cheryl Richardson

48. Festive Finance

Incredible though it may seem, Christmas really is just around the corner. Even without knowing how many 'shopping days' there are to go, I'm sure it's a terrifyingly small number. Inevitably, it's a very expensive time of year, and in the heat of the moment it's easy to spend more than we can really afford.

Here's a tip to help ensure there are some extra funds available for the Festive Season.

Do you know how much you spend in a week or a month? Do you know what you spend your money on? One way to keep tabs on this is to keep a Spending Log for a week or two – just to see where your hard-earned money is actually going. You might be in for a few surprises.

A friend of mine tried this out and was shocked to discover that she was spending, on average, £12 a week on Cappuccinos – that's a whopping £48 per month.

Another was equally shocked to realise he had a wine bill approaching £120 per month.

By becoming aware of how you're spending your money, you can take control of it. You can then decide whether to forego a Latte or two in order to have the extra funds you need to afford something special – or, more importantly, to avoid going into the red over the Holiday Season.

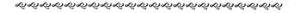

"There is nothing you can say in answer to a compliment. I have been complimented myself a great many times and they always embarrass me – I always feel that they have not said enough."

Mark Twain

49. Receiving Compliments

Whenever anyone gives us a compliment, we have a choice whether to respond assertively or unassertively. For example:

Compliment: "Your hair looks really good today."

> Unassertive Response: "That's only because I've just been to the hairdresser's!"

> Assertive Response: "Thanks, I'm pleased with it as well."

Some people find it awkward to receive compliments and tend to do the following:

1. Respond with a put down:

> "You wouldn't say that if you saw me at home," or

> "Well, it's about time I got something right, isn't it?"

2. Dismiss the compliment:

> "Oh, I've had this jacket for years," or

> "It wasn't very difficult anyway."

3. Smother the compliment immediately with a 'retaliation':

> "You do just as good a job as I do."

(Examples taken from the book 'Super Confidence' by Gael Lindenfield).

For the next week, become aware of how you respond to compliments.

If you tend towards any of the responses above, make a point of responding assertively to any compliment you may receive. It doesn't have to be complicated or over-effusive. Often a simple 'thank you' and a smile is all that's needed.

"In our African language we say 'a person is a person through other persons.' ...

We are made for a delicate network of relationship, of interdependence. We are meant to complement each other. All kinds of things go horribly wrong when we break that fundamental law of our being."

Desmond Tutu

50. Emotional Bank Account

Those of you who have read Stephen Covey's book "The Seven Habits of Highly Effective People" will recognise this term. Covey suggests that in our relationships we build up a strong and healthy 'bank account' with others by consistently 'making deposits' through acts of kindness, consideration, honesty, keeping commitments, thoughtfulness and so on. Equally, by treating someone unkindly, criticising, breaking promises, betraying trust, your account diminishes and is in danger of becoming overdrawn.

One of the ways Covey suggests to build up your bank account with the special people in your life is through Understanding the Individual. Part of this is understanding that what might constitute a deposit for you, might not do so for them. It also means making what is important to the other person as important to you.

Covey writes: "I have a friend whose son developed an avid interest in baseball. My friend wasn't interested in baseball at all. But one summer, he took his son to see every major league team play one game. The trip took over six weeks and cost a great deal of money.

My friend was asked on his return, "Do you like baseball that much?"

"No", he replied, "But I like my son that much."

I must confess that this had a profound impact on me when I read it. For years my partner Don and I have been engaged in a bit of a power struggle over cleaning the house! A spotless house is very important to him, and I had tended to rebel when he wanted me to make more of an effort in that direction. Reading Covey's words stopped me in my tracks. Don is important to me, so his desire for a clean house suddenly became more important to me as well.

Is there some way that you can apply this to your life this week?

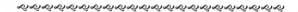

"As a silversmith sifts dust from
silver, remove your own
imbalances little by little."

The Dhammapada

51. Patterns

When we stop and think about it, we can probably recognize many different behaviour patterns in our lives. Some of these might be having a positive influence, whilst others could be doing quite the opposite. With the holiday season fast approaching, it can be valuable to take a few minutes to think about some of your behaviour patterns. Congratulate yourself on those that are likely to contribute positively to your enjoyment of the festivities – and take an honest look at those patterns which are likely to produce less positive results.

> Do you tend to run yourself ragged as a result of other people's expectations?
>
> Do you tend to eat or drink far too much over Christmas and the New Year and neglect doing any exercise?
>
> Do you take the love and support of those round you for granted?
>
> Do you over-spend and then have to spend months repairing the damage to your bank account or overdraft?

Step One: Make yourself aware of existing patterns.

Step Two: Recognize that you have a CHOICE:

a) to continue the existing pattern, or

b) to consciously let it go and adopt a new pattern that serves you better.

What NEW and IMPROVED patterns – ones that will serve you well – do you want to take with you into the New Year?

"Look not mournfully into the Past. It comes not back again.

Wisely improve the Present.

It is thine.

Go forth to meet the shadowy Future, without fear and with a manly heart."

Elaine St. James

52. Looking Back ...

As the end of the year approaches, this is a perfect time to look back and reflect on the past year.

If you can grab some quiet time between now and January 1st, why not sit down and think about everything you've achieved this year.

Write a list of all your accomplishments – large and small. You'll be surprised at how long the list will be. You might want to make this into a game involving your family or your partner.

It can be equally constructive to reflect on the things that didn't go so well – the things you were disappointed about or didn't achieve.

What lessons did you learn from these experiences?

How can you take any new awareness with you into the New Year and put it to good use when planning your year?

Wishing you a happy and peaceful Festive Season and all good things in the year to come!

References

Books

Feel the Fear and Do It Anyway, Susan Jeffers,
  published 1987, by Random House Books.

Wishcraft – How to get what you really want, Barbara Sher,
  published 1979 by Ballantine Books (a division of Random
  House.)

First Things First, Stephen R Covey,
  published 1994 by Simon and Schuster.

Leadership from the Inside Out, Kevin Cashman,
  published 2000 by Executive Excellence Publishing.

Your Best Year Yet, Jinny S Ditzer,
  published 1994 by Thorsons.

The Procrastinator's Handbook, Rita Emmett,
  published 2001 by Fusion Press (a division of Satin
  Publications Ltd).

7 Habits of Highly Effective People, Stephen R Covey,
  published 1989 by Simon and Schuster.

Super Confidence, Gael Lindenfield,
  published 1989 by Thorsons.

Coaches Mentioned

Mark Forster – The Time Freedom Coach
  Tel: +44 (0)1403-250016 www.markforster.net

Mark's books
  Get Everything Done and Still Have Time to Play (2000)
  and *How To Make Your Dreams Come True* (2002) are
  published by Hodder & Stoughton.

'Verbal Paper Cuts' and 'Take A Break!' are based on original
  articles by Bernice Ross and Byron Van Arsdale
  www.Teleclass4U.com